Diane Glancy teaches creative writing and Native American literature at Macalaster College in St. Paul, Minnesota. Her third book of poetry, *Iron Woman* (1990), was awarded the Capricorn prize by The Writers Voice, and *Trigger Dance* (1990), a collection of short fiction, won the Charles and Mildred Nilon Fiction Award from the University of Colorado and the Fiction Collective. She has been a Newberry Library and NEA fellow. Her fourth collection of poems, *Lone Dog's Winter Count*, was published in 1991.

Claiming Breath

Winner
of the
1991
North
American
Indian
Prose
Award

Award Committee

Gerald Vizenor, Chairman
University of California at Berkeley

Paula Gunn Allen
University of California at Los Angeles

N. Scott Momaday
School of American Research, Santa Fe

A. LaVonne Brown Ruoff
University of Illinois at Chicago

Claiming Breath

Diane Glancy

University of
Nebraska Press
Lincoln and London

Library of
Congress Cataloging-in-
Publication
Data. Glancy, Diane.
Claiming breath /
Diane Glancy. p. cm.
ISBN 0-8032-2140-1
1. Indians of North Amer-
ica – Literary
collections. I. Title.
PS3557.L294C58 1992
818'.5409 – dc20
91-24637 CIP

Contents

Acknowledgments

ix   Grateful acknowledgment is made to the following pub-
lications for the selections that first appeared in their
pages: *The And Review* for 'March 2 \ Portrait of Evening
Light'; *Born at the Crossroads: Voices of Mixed Heritage
Women* for 'Ontology & the Trucker'; *Calyx* for 'Decem-
ber 1 \ Fragments \ Shards'; *Cincinnati Poetry Review* for
'29th Street, Indianapolis & Far Out across the Indiana
Fields'; *Contemporary Native American Cultural Issues*
(Conference on the Native American, Lake Superior State
University) for Part 1 of 'The Nail-down of Oral Tradition';
Diarist Journal for 'December 23 \ Alia Bowman,' 'Decem-
ber 24 \ Before Dawn,' 'January 13,' 'January 21,' 'February
17,' 'February 19,' and 'November 24 \ The Chrome of
Passing Fenders'; *Hiram Poetry Review* for 'Astoria Boule-
vard'; *House on Via Gombito: An Anthology of Women's
Travels* (New Rivers Press) for 'Ontology & the Trucker';
Mid-America Review (Bowling Green State University) for
'Ethnic Arts: The Cultural Bridge'; *Mirage* for 'January 16 \
Tomatos'; *Muse, Feminist Journal* (Macalester College) for
'SHEdonism'; *Seneca Review* for 'Furniture'; *Sulfur* for
September \ Peru, Kansas' and 'April'; *A View from the Loft*
for 'February \ The Iron Cranberry' and 'Claiming Breath';
and *Waves* for 'Escarpment' and 'Against Dark Clouds.'
In addition, 'A Confession or Apology for Christian Faith'
was presented at the Great Plains Theological Seminar at
United Tribes College in Bismark, North Dakota, May 11–
12, 1991.

Special thanks go to the University of Iowa for the Equal Opportunity Fellowship and the Edwin Piper Memorial Fellowship. I am also grateful for grants from the National Endowment for the Arts and the Minnesota State Arts Board.

Claiming Breath

Teraz możemy składać wyznania bez obawy,
że zrobią z nich użytek wrogowie potężni.
Now we can make confession, without fear
that it will be used by enemies.

Czeslaw Milosz, 'The Wormwood Star'

(*The Separate Notebooks*)

I often write about being in the middle ground between two cultures, not fully a part of either. I write with a split voice, often experimenting with language until the parts equal some sort of a whole. I would say a pencil is a buffalo migration under the sky with its stars turning like a jar-lid poked with holes. Writing affects my life, my Real life, while the rest spins through the lone pines. I write from everyday circumstances, old ordinary life, and the stampede of the past. I like to see words, their friendly orifices.

December 23 \ *Alia Bowman*

1   I could relate to her those long afternoons she talked about
her husband. She'd married the wrong man, she said. There
was another man she'd almost married, but for some reason at the last, chose Elmer. She relived some of their
marriage with bitterness he'd not been a good husband. His
disregard for her in buying the truck stop & fruit farm. It
was always more work for her. He flew small planes, at one
time had a fleet of school buses, drank himself stupid. I
knew what she said. I had married her grandson, a hard
drinking Irishman, the image of his grandfather. I knew
neglect, his disregard for my feelings. She & I spent long
afternoons peeling apples, rolling out dough, thinking yes,
how we'd married the wrong man.

2   I light the candles on a small, tin Christmas tree I bought one year in Santa Fe. The smell of sulphur reminds me of the farm. A pig, a bear, a dog, a mule, & an angel made by one of the children when they were small, hang from the tree. A few bright flowers also painted on the flat tin. Dried leaves rattle on the ground outside the door. The candles flicker when the heat comes on. I watch them with plea- sure before the children get up & we drive to Kansas City for Christmas eve & day. My mother is ill, my father dead. My brother & his family come from Iowa, driving 300 miles south the same time we travel 300 north from Okla- homa. Yesterday afternoon, I had an argument with my former mother-in-law over the children driving another 100 miles to see her on Christmas morning. If she had not interfered through the years, we might still have been there as a family. But after nearly 20 years of marriage, & several years of divorce, there is nothing I miss about him. I write a fiery letter to my former mother-in-law about her unfair judgments. Blessed are the peacemakers comes into my head. All the unhappy trips to see her. All the Christmases I sat in the living room with the children while she & my former husband talked, or had it out in the other room. I was always alone with him, never anyone I could be with. I tear up the letter. Why am I happy before this tin Christ- mas tree with its flowers & uncertain flames?

December 25

3   At dusk on the way back to Tulsa, the lighted combine in
the Kansas field, the eerie flurry of dust where it paddle-
wheels the winter crop. An angel flying over some blessed
birth. On this night, I pass the earth, join my father in
space, the hose of angels, the two that came for him the
night he died. Yo tatos. I hear the whuzz of frogs flying by \
why do we meet on this busy corner this remote night? I
pass thru Kansas all my life.

December 26

4   I also want to explore the breakdown of boundaries between the genres. This 'communal' stance is inherent
in the Native American heritage. The non-linear non-
boundaried non-fenced open-prairied words. Non-creative
fiction, nearly. It's something that's there. I don't have to
make it up with the imagination. Just think of the relationships.

I want to explore my memories & their relational aspects
to the present. I was born between 2 heritages & I want
to explore that empty space, that place-between-2-places,
that walk-in-2-worlds. I want to do it in a new way.

The word is important in Native America tradition. You
speak the path on which you walk. Your words make the
trail. You have to be careful with words. They can shape
the future. For instance, when a brave hunted a bear, he
first drew the bear with his arrow in it, then when he went
hunting, the hunt was merely a result of what he'd already
done in his drawing.

December 27 \ Delay

5   From the window I hear a squirrel bark at some intrusion. I think the cat must be in the tree again. Waiting to get from one place to another. A newspaper with a crease folded into it. Waiting for piano lessons & dance lessons, waiting for the kids to clear out, waiting for my time to come. What are you anxious about? He would ask. Your chance will come when you aren't expecting it. You'll have an instant to grab onto it, running with all the baggage you can't let go of. What do you have to write about anyway?

December 28 \
Writers' Conference in Tucson

6   The plane is in the air, poking the sky with its nose. The windows like a row of corn on a cob. Because the flight was canceled yesterday, I'm in a front seat on the plane from Dallas. I, who ride the bus, who drive my old car across Oklahoma, drive thru Kansas to Kansas City, whose ancestors walked to Indian Territory behind the soldiers. Why did I marry at all? Because I could curl up again as a girl, say to my husband what I said to my father? Why was it oppressive? A yoke for which I was not fit. Why didn't I know what it would be like? I had seen my mother hurt, but it wouldn't happen to me.

December 29

7 Some tools of writing are the rhythm of language, the imagery & the thought conveyed. Out west, the frontier is on the edge of form. Not shape, but structure & organization of the writing. It is tribal, this hybrid & unfamiliar of the familiar. It's the part that comes from not belonging. Bawks. Words push into the new sphere. Tribal means belonging, but not belonging to civilization. This is the tension that results.

January 2

8 Caught in the storm of return. Everything stacked up. The floor of Tucson. Why does it stick with me? Because it's the problem of writing. The plain grit I start from. Yucca & saguaro in surrender. The desert is the synthesis. The aftermath of war. Writing is a dance of words. The shape of motion. It's field seeds on my socks. The overall movement of the field in my head. Writing sees into the night with the clarity of day. It's life force & the shifts of the moon—The feet, the loping arms, the core of imagination. Writing is word-cloth over disembodied meaning. Hohokum & Anasazi, the ancient ones who are gone. It must have that vehicle & the visions which take courage to live. Writing cannot exist without form. It's the movement of dance. Language converted into meaning with the grace of the gift transferred.

9 Something passes more than I am aware of. A truth that goes on. The wholeness of writing that emerges from the fragments. Bedrock thrust up by immeasurable pressures in the context of human life. The syntax torn as readily. A slash now & then to separate the thoughts.

January 9

10 Sometimes anger is the pestle I use to disrupt my work. My son in college, my daughter out somewhere. My former husband in another state with a new wife. I have the feeling that I, with lesser resources, must do more with them. My daughter angry sometimes that the family broke up, & now she doesn't have what she did. Well, we had it once & it didn't mean much to any of us. As a wife, I always felt clerped.

Ontology & the Trucker \ or,
The Poem Is the Road

I am Artist-in-Residence for both State Arts Councils of Oklahoma & Arkansas. Across the top of the adjoining states, there are 849 miles. I travel up & down & back & forth. On this particular trip, I am returning to Tulsa from Arkadelphia, some 250 miles. The largest part of my work seems the travel, & the loneliest part of the road is when there is no trucker.

This is a tribute for truckers who like to be followed. They are the ones who, if you show the slightest whit of intelligence about driving, let you know when to slow down & when to go fast. It's like finding broken pieces of my father along the road. Part Cherokee, intuitive, he was the surest guide I ever had.

I don't have a CB to talk to the truckers I follow. I don't want one either. There is something basic in being cut off as I travel. It reminds me I am between the way life was before I was born & how it will be after I die.

The highway is a universe where my car follows the trucks. All of us are migrating by instinct, knowing somehow where we are going. Just ahead, the sun crosses an interchange of clouds in the west, soon to exit Arkansas for the day.

I remember once on the way from Oklahoma City, there were three truckers passing, & wind blowing so hard when they passed, it shook the car and blew my papers across the seat. I keep a journal of what I pass & carry books and maps & papers with me. & out of those three truckers, I chose one to follow all the way up the hundred miles of Turner Turnpike. When we got past the toll gate at Tulsa, I turned off on the road to my house. I waved to him as we parted. It has to be that way. There's no permanency here except the highway & toll gates & road construction.

I just think how I had to say good-bye to someone I didn't want to & how everything has to move on & I didn't have any choice. That's the way it is cut off from relationships, left with the memories of them. But these ghosts are always here. I feel surrounded by them yet not really attached.

The trucks & the dotted line on the road are more real than the shadows & dreams that wait in their own world, sometimes breaking thru in poems or the last of the red sky that roams over western Arkansas. & in the dark you see more clearly sometimes if you look off to the side. That's where the poem is. You've been at a school for a week trying to tell them that, talking about poetry & why you do it, & just what it is you do. It's a long haul no matter what you pull. Might as well make it something that counts.

Might as well open this rectangle of the prairie as though it were a paragraph. Light up your truck for the dark. Name your words. Paste your meaning on like mud flaps. That's how you get thru the universe.

Now the car lights come toward you, just as white as the crack of moon through the clouds, & the trucker ahead of you isn't going fast enough because you want to get on home. It's been a long time & the mail is stacked up & the cat is lonely & you have to see how your daughter is getting along because you don't think she's old enough to get along without you all week, even though she says she is.

& you don't want to think of the week behind you because finally it is over. Soon you'll be home safe as long as a trucker's ahead of you & moving about the speed you want to go. I can't keep up with the fast ones. My car is too old & I am not that daring. I leave the slow ones behind. Soon another will come. It always does.

I remember once coming back to Oklahoma from Kansas City. My mother had been sick. & along about Pittsburg, Kansas, there was storm like we have out here—one that sweeps down from the Rockies or up out of the southwest with nothing but a few scrawny trees & a Hereford or two in Kansas or Texas to give it any resistance. I couldn't see the hood of my car for the torrents of rain & was thinking about surgery & pain & the end of life & what do we live for anyway? & thinking that maybe in the storm would be a chariot that would swoop me up to the glory these churches preach & suddenly there was a truck ahead of me & all I could see was his red taillights across the back of his truck & I held on to those lights for miles through that storm, not pulling off the road because I didn't know what was there. I was on the other side of Pittsburg when I could see the road again & I passed him—went right by like he hadn't done a thing for me. You've got to be tough.

If I had a CB, sometimes I imagine we would discuss the nature of being as we peddle along the road after dark when

I am thru gathering images. The prairie is chuck-full of them. I fill my notebooks on the seat beside me. Even after dark sometimes, things come—old visions my Indian ancestors left along the road—

Soon I stop at an all-night gas station & buy jelly beans to stay awake those miles across the prairie. I ignore any trucker who might be there. Our road game is a silent one, as though we were lovers who could not speak in public. As though our game did not exist at all. Then I just keep going again on the highway as though I took off with my poems from this prairie out into the skies thru the swinging door of the moon. I can see the trucks up there—their lights like new constellations. I try to tell what color the jelly beans are in the dark. Pretending I'm farther along the road than I am.

& those ministers come on the radio with blessed Jesus carrying the burden of his cross. & I think that must be what we are doing right here on this road, carrying our load of words across the Arkansas River with this weight of hope & despair & earning a meager living & not being overloaded for weight stations.

Finally, the Oklahoma border & I'm back in my own state to one toll gate after another. I bite into a jelly bean, & if it is an orange one I don't like, I throw it out for the gophers—careful so the car won't get splattered—

That old black jelly bean sky when there are no stars out—they've all been gathered up & hauled to the roller rink in one of those twinking towns you see along the highway—

FINALLY! Two trucks pull onto the road & behind them a whole convoy of trucks signaling to one another, flashing their lights when it's all right to pull back in—mud flaps dancing—War-painted braves! From the back, the trucks look like large ice-cube trays & beyond them you see the skinny line of highway barrels lined up for miles on the road & you know how far you have to go.

Better than one truck is two truckers who want you to follow between them. It's called 'riding the cradle.' My sister-in-law told me that when we were on our way to Iowa. Just act like you can hold your own on the road & they take you on as worthy to travel with them. How could I tell them they represent the poem for me?— Or the process of the poem—pursuing the organization, the form & energy of it. Or they represent, anyway, what I've found about writing here on the prairie— How much of it is actually a matter of attitude & vision.

& following them, the struggle of migration across the prairie is a little easier. Then the trucks become the ancient herds of buffalo the tribes followed—returned just as the fathers prayed they would—thick & fat—& the buffalo-burger is over the fire, so to speak. & the lights of oncoming cars thru the median grasses flicker, then dance again like a ghost tribe & you hear the words—'Hey yey hey yey'—coming from your mouth & finally, FINALLY, the miles go by.

Soon my turnoff comes & I hate to leave my place between the two trucks. I have the last 70 miles without them & I wave. Good-bye— It's like before you were born when god

says, 'see ya,' & you can never hear him again in this life
but you know he's there with you on the road late at night
when you're tired from working & on several hundred
miles of your way home. That's mostly the way it is out
16   here following a trucker who wants you to follow— You
see him go on west, maybe Amarillo or Albuquerque or
even the coast still 1,500 miles away, while you turn north
& watch the trucks disappear & you feel that thread, that
invisible twine like words that somehow hold us all
together—

January 10

17   I will not be outdone. Hold the book on the edge of the chair. Read the sweep of words out of the wigwam. Sweep. Sweep. Migration of language from blue trees \ the leaves whirl at the window \ into the field of houses. Closed in \ some days work thru the morn \ thru afternoon into evening until stunned as a deer in sudden headlights, I stand at the bed. Sometimes there was a cabbage & a potato to eat. An onion & a feather blown at the window. Bare words one by one out of the head into air \ their regiments holding the gorge.

January 12 \ Glotto

18 A war zone in the old neighborhood where I grew up in
Kansas City. Some of the houses boarded & no one goes out
at night. Once in a while we drive by the house when I am
back in Kansas City. My mother holds to her side of the
seat, saying, they shoot you here. I remember walking up
the gentle hill to a friend's who had a play-kitchen under
her back porch. We made supper of berries & twigs & took
turns with dishes. Down the street, in my yard, there was
only an open space the harsh sun burned each summer.
Out across the plains, the round, irrigated fields from a
plane would look like burners on a stove. Maybe that's
why I'm always looking for a place. My one buffalo dress,
one string of hides.

January 13

19   Words are not my inheritance. My Cherokee grandmother could not write. My father finished grade school. When his father died, he migrated north from Viola, Arkansas, to Kansas City & worked in the stockyards. My mother got farther in school before she went to Kansas City to live with an uncle, who was a Methodist minister. She would always be a housewife & my father worked for the packing house all his life. My childhood breached the space between them. Those dark nights closed in the bungalow on Fiftieth Terrace \ a cave with a living room drawn on the wall, large trees, & a west sun like a searchlight from the front porch.

January 14 \
It's My Kitchen under the House

20   Between petroglyph & written language \ the intermediary \
itself a state. Writing from the past \ fragments of memory \
the way language first sounds to someone who is not used
to it. Cracks in the strata of mountains \ we don't see often
in the prairie \ but in Tucson the past got thru \ & lonely
planets in cold space revolving around the sun. Mumal \ a
mural of new worlds made.

January 16 \ Tomatos

21   A string of tamoots \
break into them \ spurt
green sleeds \ gerzy.
A tribe of matoots.
Constellations \ their scattered feathers.
Look into the black space of buffalo.
Language neighs in the krummholz
& static electricity gerps the prairie
with afterburn.
Warriors once more squeeching their war whoops
slide down the cords of lightning
back to dance in prairie ooze \
ototams tied to their loins.
They slip through when the wind is up.
Winter magnatism. Matotos.
Umbrageous woods of space \
a string of fish hangs from their braids.
I think they prefer the prairie
to the south coast of the stars.
Red skinned \ ottomas.

January 17

22 My inheritance is the Arkansas backhill culture mixed with Cherokee heritage. That's only my father's side. My mother's people were Kansas farmers of German & English descent. So the slow, backwoods illiteracy I inherited received the will & order & persistence of the anglo culture. (All things which I resent in my mother). I find this Indian side moving backward & the white side moving forward, both at the same time tendered by the isolation of the prairie. Sometimes I hear my ancestors speak their riffled language. When spellings are not understood, the confusion opens the way for new combinations & misreadings of the words. Maybe this strain of writing retreats to some primeval core before it moves on.

January 20

23 Writing is the hammer & chisel that breaks down the established way of thinking. A concrete event, then an abstraction. An image, then a thought. Finally, writing builds another establishment with the fragments. I would like to go farther, but feel I must make use of myself as a found object. Sometimes I would read my writing & he got that look on his face like he'd taken a bite of something he was unfamiliar with, & didn't know what to do with it. Say it quickly, he told me. They won't listen for long.

January 21

24 The days I get along on nothing. Peanut butter scraped from a jar. Crackers. The days I am alone writing the mammoth from a cave drawing. My sight wavy as the horns of an antelope. My mouth waters at the thought of an apple. I could give up, forget writing. But if the river dries up, I will carry the canoe, grass dance around the earth lodge. The tanned hide of winter. A turquoise sky.

January 23

25 Writing leaps outrageously \ Sagebrush in the wind. Yet at
the same time, the metaphor cements the fragments of our
broken world. & this tension \ ripping out \ building in \
U-nites the writing & holds it apart. A brother who has the
toy I want. A marriage to the wrong man. Writing keeps us
in a continual state like the earth \ Continental plates
disappearing into the core, erupting again as lava to form
new land.

February \ *The Iron Cranberry**

26   My car has over 100,000 miles. A '78 Buick station wagon. I travel for the State Arts Council. I make 600-mile round trips to visit my mother, who has had cancer now for three years. I'm always on the road, week after week.

This particular Sunday afternoon, I start out after a snow. I have a residency 200 miles straight west on Highway 51. The highway is a single-lane road, & after severe weather, usually no more than two ruts thru the snow. My heavy car has no trouble.

Oklahoma is prairie country, full of space & remoteness. After snow, I pass the white, rolling fields, a few scattered farm houses or trailers, & some trees along the road—then the flat prairie beyond them, which is the stretch of the Great Plains thru western Oklahoma. It's farm country, ranches, & what's left of the oil rigs & pumping units. They used to light up the night country like a fair. Now it's dark.

The past week, flu went through the schools & I feel it coming on. I drive into the snow blowing across the road in places, the last of the gray sun giving the frozen world a pinkish cast. At some of the churches in towns I pass, faithful members arrive for Sunday-night services.

*A name given the Canberra, a British reconaissance plane first used in World War II.

The small town where I'm going rests in a shallow valley south of the Canadian River. One café in town with farmers who stare at strangers. One motel—a Butler building on the raw edge of the two-block town. I carry in my box of school materials & my clothes for the week. Unpack my things in the room. There's a hole in the plaster of the wall. Also a television, a table & crooked lamp, a bed & phone.

In the night the storm comes back. I shiver under the thin covers in my robe & nightgown & socks. Finally I get my coat & put it over me too. Morning comes & there is no school. I walk across the hard street between the ice patches with the wind blowing straight out of New Mexico & Texas. Have breakfast with the farmers staring at me, & shuffle back across the street. I go to bed again.

The next day, I go to school. At 3:30, I return to the motel room & stay there until the next morning, broken only by dinner in the café. I forgot my decaf tea bags & drink hot water, which seems to go with my residency in western Oklahoma. I feel weak again from the flu, alone on the flat prairie where the weather could incarcerate me again. I'm a stranger in town, worse than a stranger. By then, the farmers know I'm a poet. I sit looking out the window at the cold, hard street. The trucks parked with their noses to the curb like cows at the water trough. The hard ice with dirty patches of water underneath. My car, covered with dried highway slush, looks like a huge cranberry in front of my room at the motel.

I always feel like I work in isolation. Walking into one class after another, talking about contemporary poetry— It's not what they think it's going to be. It doesn't rhyme. What's this I'm giving them? I read one poem after another. I tell them poetry is a distilled experience, not the flowery language it used to be. I have many writing exercises I give. Usually, something magic happens, & the students write poems with clarity & detail. They share them before the class if they choose. If not, they don't have to.

I write whenever I can on these residencies. Sometimes, if there is enough studio time during the day, I take my work to school & write where they can see me. The point being I do it because I want to—& the discipline it takes.

I feel a responsibility to my words. Poetry is road maintenance for a fragmented world which seeks to be kept together. It's been an integral activity for a long time. I travel through wind storms, the summer heat & winter blizzards—all the harsh elements of the prairie. Yet I find there's also a refinement to the region. The vast unspeaking prairie: the poet only has to gather the words. The AUTHORity of the written word & I seek MORE—

With my car, that is. I couldn't go anywhere without it. Nor my faith in Christ. Always on these harder residencies when I feel I'm the only one in the universe, Christ is the rope I hang on to. That faith has never failed me. Who could travel with less?

I also have this tall grass prairie, this prayer-ee for my territory & always in travel, in the act of migration, is the POEM. The holy word is foundation for our civilization. I think that's why I like to travel. It doesn't always matter where. As long as my car runs.

I spend the week in a building with students from first grade thru high school. Several of the rooms in the basement have no windows. In another room, there's a bowl with a few small dinosaur bones found nearby in the valley south of the Canadian. I ask if I can have one. I always collect rocks & weeds & found objects from my travels, as well as images to write with.

It was on that residency I was asked to finish a rhyming cheer for a basketball game in the next town—if the weather held.

I think poetry evolves out of ordinary circumstance—the ideas I write about often come from the hardness of prairie life. Somehow I still make notes after a week of poetry. Words are integral to existence, especially after a week with hardly anyone to talk to. There seems to be something inaccessible about being the visiting artist. Not so much with the kids in the classroom. They often have a myriad of questions.

I share my life in the classrooms—what I do as a writer, the confining routine, the struggle to make a living. The miles I have on my car. I tell them it takes tenacity to send out poems consistently & receive little or no remuneration for the work. At least one day, I wear my *Iowa Review* T-shirt—'Thank you for sending us your work. We are sorry that we cannot use it & that the volume of submissions precludes a more personal reply.'

They seem to know. These are the progeny of the sod farmers who staked their claim during the land runs, & the hay farmers who got blown away in the dust bowl. These are children of the farmers who struggle now. One of them told me that poetry must be like farming.

I think about the kids in the classrooms who brought me their poems, who asked questions, who dared to share themselves. I often see them tremble as they read their work. They are the ones who hear the inner voice & don't know what to do with it yet. They get away from generalities into details & feelings. They have respect for words & see them open before them like soil under a plow.

I think of the resentful students too, who slouch in their chairs in the back of the room, who finally give me two lines that are a flashlight into the darkness where they live. They have known failure all their lives, & finally express it with the written word.

Then on Friday, I pack my things in the motel room where I spent five long evenings & nights with a banging heater & bare walls. I pay $94 of my $500 paycheck to the motel, & start on the road back to Tulsa. Finishing a residency is like being a rubber band shot across the prairie. It's like one of those spitwads I see flying over the classrooms sometimes— It's low flight in my car back east on Highway 51.

Easier residencies followed that year. In May in another town, 30 miles farther west on Highway 51, the students gave me a cache I hope always to have with my dinosaur bone and prairie images: a heart made from red pipe cleaner, filled with colored 'fuzz balls,' & an artificial brown velvet leaf sticking out the top. Handmade crosses & cards. A letter from Jesus purchased at a local grocery. Flowers picked from yards just before the sun scorched them. All sorts of handwritten notes—

I want to think you for coming to my school. I learned a lot from you. I hope you come back next year. I had a lot of fun. You are the best poet I ever saw in my entire life. P.S. Write me back. Then I will write you back.

Thank you for comming this week. I really enjoyed you and your poens. I like what you said some people do not like you but I want you to know that I liked it. Oh I wanted to tell you ever time this week you came in you really looked nice. Well I have to go now.

I thank you for your time you spent on me and my fellow puipls I will rember this week forever and you to!!

February 17

32 When they called & told me my house had been broken into, I was silent on the phone. Far away, not able to get there, I couldn't think of anything to say. I listened as they told me of drawers pulled out & turned over on the floors, room after room. The back window broken. I couldn't even say turn down the thermostat so the cold air doesn't make the furnace run all the time. I didn't think about the television nor typewriter. But my jewelry, not much, only a few pieces leftover from a marriage, was now gone. I thought of thieves pulling out my belongings in a heap, looking for something not theirs to sell. Most of what I have is mine— A wooden high chair, a cow skull, a kerosene lamp that was my mother's when she was a girl, rocks, weeds, my poetry books & manuscripts. Scraps of words no one would want.

February 19

33 Finally I'm on my way home. The house is waiting like a
child who's been hurt. I think of my son when he was hit
by a rock at camp & I had to meet him on the road, take
him for stitches. But this is just a house. Once I yelled at
my daughter for rearranging my towel closet, getting it out
of whack so I couldn't find the sewing basket, the yard
stick, the important things. Now I pay toll at the turnpike
gate, travel a few more miles. I open the door & see the television is gone, the cushions moved off the sofa. Drawers
open in the dining room, drawers pulled out on the floor in
my bedroom. My typewriter is still there. Empty earring
boxes scattered on the floor. My jewelry box is gone. Shoe
boxes in the closet pulled down— I don't have a stereo or
VCR they look for. They shouldn't expect much from a
writer. The remote control for the television is gone from
the table when I go back to the living room. The weeds &
rocks I collect are there. Some tools from my grandfather's
farm, his straight blade, ice pick, my grandmother's butter
molds. But my great-grandfather's leather pouch of buck-
shot is gone. He carried it thru the Civil War. It's the only
thing I can't replace. The rest—a shower curtain? Police
say it's how they carried the stuff out. Cabinet doors in the
kitchen stand open. The basement door. I go down to look.
Something is gone. Later I realize it's the box my television
came in—carried off with the TV in it, as though they came
with a purchase order—as though it were really theirs.

March 2 \ *Portrait of Evening Light*

34   Maybe the shadows stay open too late. After a long day you find it's still not over. The avenue thru the trees, the race at stop lights. Once the full moon broke into the house. Windows danced. But now the past returns. You still can see thru the trees. Put them together. The twilight taking the hedge. Pieces of the yard. The slow flight of birds unzipping the lawn.

March 7 \ *Because It Should Be Done*

35 Were they friends, sharing the dark of the flowered bedroom, the invisible white of sheets she hung on the line?
Was the window open that June night as they sweated,
clung together? It was time. They had crept thru the depression, saved for a house, collected chairs & spoons, a
silver meat fork. The new decade shined straight as
clothesline under the moon. It all pointed to a family. A
knife-sharpened pencil on the table. A packet of zinnia
seeds for the narrow yard between the houses. Later, they
fell into that space between the clothesline, pale as freezer
burn. But then—back in that time, was there noise between them as they loved? Possibly only the walnut bed in
its upheaval—the rest of the time silent as the child they
worked for.

Old Mother

36   Her bladder swells like a pond after rain. Surgery just ahead
will be like pulling weeds and tying back tomatoes. Buck
up, old mother. It starts to get dark. These pasture fences
are staves of music flying by the car. Notes gone. I hold the
bunches of field weeds to her chest now that shadows
extend across the road.

Escarpment

37 House on the butte protected against the bugs I drive
against at night, thick on the windshield in the morning. I
wait for the tests \ wait to hear \ build up layer after layer.

It is not that simple, or this that requires more of us than it
did of them. More than dwelling in the plains these first
houses buttes in themselves \ it was more than \ year after
year until our sod house was Indian mound buried inside \
cast-iron crib, a chest of drawers, shard, kettle, hoe, the last
of the green beans, a few brown hens.

Backed into a hill \ escarpment under the trawl of clouds I
reach up \ harsh plains left us raising the farm from preda-
tors \ the flare of cooking fires.

Heat wakes early here. Wind in loose boards of the house \
the blizzard of her breathing. Death of the sky pink as a
row of azaleas \ death of the woman in the next bed. Flower
pots in window boxes above us shoveling the earth \ always
moving to a higher ground.

Against Dark Clouds

38 Low white clouds lifted by wind are like smoke from grass fire. Striped road signs graze until they, too, smell the smoke & rush panicked with the car. A dull green truck with two close red eyes watches as I reach through the dark & pull it behind me. Now I drive toward the cattle truck as though it were a barn I could drive into. No, an ark losing animals. In this dim green light of dusk, the oncoming cars unfold & grow large like flocks of stampeding animals.

Not alone together since we shared a room, my brother & I stand at her bed. It's the edge of death we walk all our lives, climbing from one level to the next, renewed & different, yet something of the past remains: the edge of smoke from the next hill, the small, small distance where we once played.

Last Bath

39 She gets down into the bathtub & can't get up. Not enough strength in her legs, she can't bend them under her to rise & I can't lift her. I let the water out, call my aunt. She comes & together we lift her. First on a stepstool in the tub, then up. She moans at first, cries out. It's the shoulder she broke when she fell last winter & I'm holding her up with it. I can't let go, but hold on until she feels she can stand, her warm, damp body soon a lump on the bed. We dry her, dress her. Her body shriveling, her legs drawn up under her, her arms folding into her chest.

April

40 Just turning out one fork was all she could do at the end.
She rested all day for that one chore & when I visited she
rallied for a moment & sank into the rest of the evening.
The mind puts its body in another room. Shuffs it off as a
child. Orphaned. Goes on to meet whatever's there. The
house with its difficult furniture & border at the ceiling.
We practiced farewell in the overstuffed room. Ordinary
chat in the drive, the dear legs of the china cabinet, gaudy
glasses that plague the memory. Radio, garish bric-a-brac.
The blade of her complaining whittled the flowers on the
wall. The white schmoo of the washer in the basement.
Tools for biscuits. The fridge with its brain coiled above its
shoulders. Beds in the other room bought with the care of
surgery. Out of one meal after another letting the routine
separate the stove that heats the sun passing over it. Erupting pintos & mashed potatoes going & coming back the
jump of sun & shade on the rug. The meat hammer, the
flour blood-stuck to the paper. The words like landscapes I
heard at the dining-room table.

Migration to Summer Camp

41 Now it's her again & I make-trip from Tulsa to Kansas
City, 300 miles north. My mother had one kidney re-
moved. Now she spreads under the cobalt sky. All summer
I will drive thru Kansas, past cornflowers & Queen Anne's
lace in fields & scattered towns: Parsons, Pittsburgh, Fort
Scott.

Many years we were separated by distance & old argu-
ments. We are scarred as the strip mines I pass, different as
Queen Anne's lace & cornflowers. She is Anglo & I have
the Indian blood buried in my father's heritage.

I'm impatient with her weakness & feel the bitterness I
carry for her. For every step I took, it seemed she pushed
me down. Now she struggles to rise & it is only with help
& grimacing that she sits in a chair for a while.

I know the bends & hollows of the old highway where we
traveled to my grandfather's farm when I was a child. I pass
the old road to his farm, the road to the cemetery where the
family is buried, & the drugstore where we stopped.

Haybales are headstones in the fields, & clouds flower the
Hume cemetery where the family straddled the Missouri-
Kansas border.

There is anger still between us. But now in storms I
hear the prayer song as tribes migrated to summer camp-

grounds. Lightning bolts in one field are crooked stems of wheat leaping back to earth.

In Bucyrus, I see Christ's steeple above the trees. I feel sympathy for the first time & she, for once, is glad I am there. I wipe her as she did me when I was small. I hold the crossed trails of white settlers & Indians, endure two heritages, & in these trips, the healing of our tribes.

Agnes and Rachel

43 2 old women share a room across the hall. Rachel, the dominant, & Agnes, pitiful child with white hair & mouth open in horror. I'm sick of looking at you, Rachel fusses at Agnes. Turn off the light. Not that way, you stupid shit. The switch is by the towels. With short, raspy voice Rachel orders Agnes all day. We hear her voice across the hall. Then Rachel's hospitalized & we think sweet relief for Agnes, but she's alone & her look of horror intensifies. A woman pushes another up the hall. Come in, Agnes says. You can sleep here tonight. She pulls the wheelchair woman in her room, shoos out the woman who walks, leaves the door ajar. Soon we see Agnes start to undress the paralyzed woman. The housedress open, nearly off. The woman can't get away from Agnes, the child undressing a doll to sleep with, while mother's gone from the dark corners of her heart.

Another Morning
at the Nursing Home

44   A sudden voice startles us from nodding. Some old man with rubber soles on the linoleum after the mop goes by, the breakfast cart, someone pulling cellophane off a roll.

The slow traffic of the bowels. The nurse comes in with rubber gloves, sticks her hand up the rectum, says there's nothing but the body consuming itself. The slick balls of gas bulb the air for a while.

Someone shrieks from her room. An old man breathes through the shut door of his lungs. The rest shuffle by the door. These white people, skulls with sunken eyes and open mouths. Chimpanzees on their way to the dining hall.

I stand in the door waiting for her tray. Somewhere under her matted eyelids the small blue china dishes of her eyes.

Flight #673

45   The plane bursts from Pittsburgh into herds of clouds. Blanched rhinos, giraffes. Lions stealthy as the transported Congo. I go back to the leafy walks at the zoo when my fingers reached for the bears while mother killed an afternoon.

South of Cleveland, the sky's clear as the time I understood essence moves from one form to another. Long ago we prowled the corners of our cage, expelling bars with imagination.

Now a 5-hour delay in Chicago, watching antelope graze the distant veld. My mother in the hospital again, & I trying to get to her, trying for some connection to the past when we were not bothered by plane delays, nor death, never thinking of the dangers we escaped in the world.

Morning Light

46 Sometimes you wake from sleep dragging the other self, the greater one you leave behind when you wake, the one who can understand what you can't. Now you face the day wearing your father's sweater with mothholes she kept in her drawer 14 years after his death, as though he'd knock again one evening. You close the book you brought with you, pass the empty bookcase, the old chair, your hide-drawings of the spirit lifting from the body. You know you still have the end to go thru. You spend your life next to her, yet find air pockets & holes. Lucretius, it's more than matter & the void where matter moves. It's Christ-faith, it has to be, & the courage, the decency you get from it. It's you joined to yourself you take with you when you're hit across the wall, a high fly into the morning light.

July 11 \ Indian Giver

47 Boxes piled to the ceiling, goblets, plates on a pile of news-
    papers, no meals spread upon them, for a while anyway. A
    mother's illness, trips to the hospital, her rapid decline.
    Clearing out her apartment, the yard falls into boxes,
    packed Indian vases from trips to Canyon Road, Santa Fe
    bear pottery. The boxes of what no one knows, other boxes
    everyone has a hold on. The dragging of cacia molbs, bird
    talleys, pitcher from the Civil War. Take two mbites, you
    fuss over her. Meanwhile your own house in upheaval,
    standing bull in the tea closet. Familiar light quarters your
    room, the routine you know all your life. Now the un-
    known faced especially by her. You wrap what you want.
    The light from long afternoons. Totums. A fragment of a
    trip to California when you looked down & the engine quit
    the only forgiveness you knew for years.

48   She steps from the stove, one foot rising to the air, the
     other still in the saucepan, up over fields, green, or brown
     as grocery sacks. The road twists dribbled milk between
     the scattered houses, the rows of gardens. Once she was
     young, the drive-in, a hand-fan spread out on a summer
     evening, a few clouds like stray children floating by.

July 16

49 The basement hung with sheets to hide the washing ma-
chine & furnace. Paper shades on bare light bulbs. Streamers. Starch-flecks from crinolines glittering on the floor. A
frosted casket on the work bench, perhaps too sugary, too
white.

August 25 \ Trinity of Landscapes

50   It was my mother's chest in back of the open truck, taking it to Tulsa after her death. The sofa & her framed watercolor under a cloudy sky.

The cedar chest now in the rain with the design of 1933 when they married. The ark of the covenant shuffled from Shiloh. The edge of the tarp waving to

1. the crowd of trees, the cows in fields.

2. The watercolor of a road past a farmhouse.

3. My memory of the farm tucked in the chest with albums of the family now dead or gone.

We wait under the underpass in the rain. Abba, Father, Lama sabachthani? The chest washed, no baptized in rain.

SHEdonism

51   I have a poem called 'Dead Wood': 'At night I hear the breath of wolves \ Eee por tay. The limbs that whack my \ head. I chop the darkness for firewood. \ Dreams tug at my head. My father's \ death, my mother's illness, my son's \ surgeries, my husband's absences. It \ would make sense to let go. But when I \ wake in the night in a sweat, still \ driving the stage to Dead Wood, I think, \ this is what it's like to be a man.' It's a prose poem so the line breaks aren't that important. But what is, is the realization that without thinking I equate a responsible human being with the male gender. And even after I've done it, it doesn't bother me enough to make me change the poem. Let it be. It says what I felt when I wrote it.

I suppose it's because I'm from a generation whose mothers were homebound. It was my father who was the center of energy for the family. While he was at work and we were at school, my fretful, punctual mother waxed floors and baked cookies. She endured her isolation with complaint if I remember correctly. For most of those years she didn't have a car and even after she did and we were grown, she still stayed at home and felt uncomfortable with the freedom to be her own person. In fact, I don't think she ever made it to herself.

It was to my benefit to learn the agonies of that journey—that pulling off of adhesive that had been stuck there so long. In my case, it happened in the very beginning. Marriage was not the 'center' for my definition of self. It was painful. My husband traveled and drank a great deal. I received no comfort from him. I had the responsibility of keeping the house and family together and I did it for 19 years, most of which I wanted to leave. I also got my M.A. and taught writing during those years. Now I'm finally on my own.

But it's not a woman's relationship to a man or the absence of that relationship that defines a woman. It's what the woman is to herself.

Being a minority also enlarged my difficulties. Maybe it's the reason I stayed married so long. I didn't know what else to do. In fact, it was all I could do for a while. I didn't fit into the structure of school. I always felt unworthy of what I wrote. It has taken YEARS to find my way. But my Native American heritage is also a strength (especially the images I get from it for writing). So my structure has always been one of conflict and ambivalence. Aren't all of us made of paradox and diversity, anger, hurt, hope, guilt, endurance? Aren't we all fragments of opposition, especially women? A composite for which we have to provide the connecting threads.

In an essay called 'Fragments \ Shards' (about the journey to the *ani-yun-wiyu*, or 'real people'), I called this existence, 'SHEdonism': the enjoyment of oneself as a woman. It includes the ability to sort through things and live with dichotomy, even in a world that has its own fragments and conflicts.

I think you can be your own person even in a situation you don't like. Many times I felt powerless at the moment as a woman with the responsibility of family and with the negative aspects of the Native American heritage, but inside, I dreamed and felt the presence of myself even when it was fretful, stressed and impatient. What I've ended up with over the years is myself as a friend.

I also learned independence as I taught writing. Isn't writing thinking? Aren't our lives made up of words? The ability to write clearly is the ability to think clearly. So I used exercises for both creative and essay or idea-transferring writing: thinking through the situation, organizing it, writing it clearly. Externalizing the thought process. Finding form for content. Using language for creative, expressive purposes. The revelation of words, their boldness, the imaginative impact of combined images, of seeing the familiar in a new way. That's what writing is. That's what living is. That's probably what feminism is.

54   Writing takes the world behind the curtain of the brain \
     does a number on it \ & WHAMMO out comes another
     dimension \ a sea within a sea in which the Titanic of our
     expectations disappears & we are left with \ What is it?

In writing, life sinks \ rises like the moon with new vis-
ibility \ another dimension \ seeing what we've not seen in
a different way than if we'd seen it.

Only poetry or a form of new writing captures the thoughts
that entomb the mind \ the disorder of memory, the un-
chronological order.

I think it's one of the purposes of art \ to hold disaster in
artistic control.

September \ Peru, Kansas

55   The creek slutes north of town, a curve, a grocery, a few houses, fence slats, then the country blozomed to the land.

Warrior & squawl with towel hanging at the car window \ edges flapping like a bird trying to take off from the land.

Out here where water's scarce cows stand in ponds to hold them down. Language starts with their breath & the hurrrr of wind around grain elevators \ space ships in their towers.

Far away, turnpike tollgates are moons of Uranus. The dark sky \ transparent at night \ but for the black-eyed rudge of trees. In Peru \ salibales of words are hayrolled in fields. Look & you will find corridors of meaning in any direction, layers of it, anything you want \ a square box, root of fields, soy beanies & weet.

You can even feel the laps of the sky's tongue on your shoes. All directions, yet the openness doesn't take the hoe handle.

You still hold your loss as though it were something. The cutting into molars \ jaw \ the cold bone-white of the skull.

Driving thru Kansas is like being married to a man you didn't fit with \ not having money \ your days full of chores & boredom \ a towel in your window to keep out the sun.

Robes of wheat whick by like crosses in a country cemetery.

You pass the unanimous bend of weeds. Just look where
they are pointing \ the openness in fields. The opundance
of language seeping to another.

Ee tabo cay moose \ Worriar & squaw \ their carwindow
flapping over shed & galvanized tanks. Step anywhere &
grasshoppers jump in the corn.

The wind flings you with dust from fields & gravel roads.
Clouds in hopeless plight to wind patterns qpurting revolt
from county line to line. Soon, the little sprats of rain on
sunflars & gutturals of old stone houses \ sheds following
like calves.

The space that sounds in brittle cornstalks is all yours \ the
hinge of bugs opening Peru \ when you beat hollyhocks
with your stick until the yard pinked with furzz & the
grandmother yelled her tomahawk language.

All language defeats \ pulls out your tongue \ strips the
loose string of bone from your back \ the bonds of ponds not
giving in to earth, but kissing the sky.

All your life you want to feel ponded to the land \ enaporat-
ing upword. The sky thumbs through the cornrows as you
pazz by head whacked off \ feet lifted from the floor in a car
going fast to get thru.

Here at the End of the Ride

57 Which is where I was in the other part of time when I called. My house broken into again. I'm two days away. My son tells me he doesn't think they took much. The new TV is gone. The rest already taken. Papers & clothes & shoes on the floor. Coke sprayed on the kitchen walls. He's not sure what else. My friend & I pass squirting waterwheels on Idaho fields. Now I'm in a hurry & miss the turn. We head straight into the mountains, the slowest way through Wyoming. I read the map but it takes too long to turn back. I feel anger at them in my house. Rodents. I imagine they come back again & I am waiting with a gun. They are dead when police arrive. On the map I find a short cut from Laramie. A winding road between boulders under moonlight. We get to Fort Collins late at night. My friend can't sleep. Takes a pill nearly at dawn. Now it's morning & he's groggy. It's time to get on the road. I once had a husband who got up, left me before I could get out of bed to grope my way through restaurants & cities where we traveled. But my friend stays in bed, mumbles he can't get up. I pack the car, get ice for the water jug, ask directions to the interstate. I go back into the room, tell him I can't wait. I pull the covers down, put his underwear on him, the undershirt over his head. I put on his socks, a shirt sleeve on one arm. He shuffles to the bathroom like an old man. His shirt collar under his sweater. He sits in the car, saying he didn't gets his money's worth from the motel. On the road, we leave Colorado & start across Kansas. We'll drive to Oklahoma far into the night.

Next Day

58   I wash the kitchen walls. Pick up papers which are knee-deep from all my files turned upside down. In the closet my shoe boxes are spilled again. I find the black and white checked dress I bought for my mother's funeral is gone. But they left the sash. A wide piece of cloth with large checks. I jerk it from the hanger. Take it to the front porch. Tie it to the post. A banner of look-what-you-forgot.

Ethnic Arts: The Cultural Bridge

59   I want to share what it's like to think as a
Native American. This will be nonlinear. There
will be no outcome. No motive. No logic. I'm
simply sharing the experience of it, the
impressions during the migration of a paper.
Maybe something in the Coyote-trickster tradition.

I started writing from a middle ground. Between
2 cultures. Looking down there was not much
under me. A blind spot where the floor didn't
meet. I pulled up some mud, put it on a turtle's
back, as the creation myth says. It grew into
land. A solid place to stay, yet capable of
movement. The dream of it traveling.

I had to communicate with the 2parts of myself
before I could reach others.
The direct line to my Indian heritage had been
lost. My father told me we were Cherokee. & there
were enough trips to the old place in Arkansas
I knew it was true. He'd left his heritage
& migrated north to Kansas City for work. But
even when the roots are severed, the beginning is
still there. I can't remember anything my Indian
grandmother said to me, yet her heritage stands
before me like a stone iceberg, a huge presence,
all the more terrible for its silence.

The artist makes a land between 2places. I
wasn't Indian having been raised separate from the
culture. I wasn't white either. There was always
a gulf between the parts of myself, & a gulf
60   between others. I had to create a place from which
to create a place.

You know how in sleep people dream.
& how during sensory deprivation we hallucinate.
I think I would define art as spiritual
hallucination.
It seems to me I am separated from the Spirit,
from God.
It seems to me I'm separated from that inner self
lost in the hurry of my days.
The impersonal mind I carry in my head
longs for the heart.

Art makes sure of it.

Art is that link between them.
Maybe in all ethnicities,
but certainly in the Native American.
The link itself a partnership
with other roller rinks
under the moving pavilion-lights of stars.

Yet there must be standards that reflect the
abutment of self to reality.
Art must connect. & we must tell our story
with the craft of form & content.

Art is important because it balances the evil powers. It's a medicine woman. A shaman.

As far as style,
often there is repetition of motifs. That repetition causes another state of mind by going over & over until the mind leaves the form & enters the movement, the process of going. Until the heart reaches the spirit it seeks. But there is another reason why repetition is maintained & that is the desperate holding on to that which is slipping away daily, & in my case already lost.

In my writings I deal with ghosts.
But they're REAL ghosts.
The-moving-of-them-in-trees.

The invisible ones struggling to become visible.
To themselves as much as others.
The tension between.
Until the holes be made whole.
& until the wholes be made hole
to see the other world.

The dependency of the incomplete & complete.
The fluidity of states.

I have a poem that begins, 'Each morning I wake invisible. I sew my feet onto my legs, lift spine

onto my thighs. All day I work with one hair
after another.' & so forth.

I think ethnic art seeks peace & resolution. The
62 naming of fragments. The sticking together of them
like the pottery bowl I bought at Two Harbors,
Minnesota, on the shore of Lake Superior last
summer. My cat knocked it off the table one night
& I put it back together with Elmer's glue.

That's what I do when I write. What ethnic group
doesn't suffer brokenness?
I read it even in the short stories of the white
writers I teach.
& who is the artist
for whom the cracks don't show?

Art is discovery of connecting threads not only
within ourselves but in the universal condition of
life. Our 'humanness' is the same whatever the
ethnic group. We just have different medicines
for carrying those differences.

For me, art is pacification & purification of
old grievances. I write about the loss of land
& I think it had to happen. Can you imagine
America remaining as it was while the rest of
the world moved on? Perhaps it could have been
handled better.

Art is healing for those left behind
when everyone else goes to school.

The Merthiolate my father used to spray in our sore
throats.
& art is healing for wounds up there
on the front line.

It's a sense of belonging & yet a sense of
individuality within the tribe.
Somehow they go together.

A sense of discovery.
We're in this human condition together.
Some have it easier than others
& it's not fair. Yet there's something about
it. I don't have the word, the concept, as yet
the movement to imagine it in dance.
But there's an inner sense seeking expression.

A discovery of the little things.
I was looking for a word one day in the dictionary
& I found 'tragus.' The prominence in front of
the external opening of the ear.
& I have two of them.

The reciprocity of the known to the unknown.
The-trees-of-them-moving-in-twigs.

Now Re: The ethnic land bridge
like the Bering Strait my ancestors migrated over
some 15,000 years ago, following the mammoth.
I would not want to raise the Strait
& go back to my Oriental origins, if that's where we
came from.

But forward into America.
I have a part of it now
& it's worth the struggle it took to get it.

64   Art as communication that says to others
you'd better listen.
Here's a message from the next country.

The expanding & contracting creative energy of
thought into outward form
which is itself a moving
entity. Already more than we can handle.
Art promises the holder won't be bored.

This is not what was but moves between the was &
will & is the always,
the line moving through the medicine of stars,
planets, the holes for eyes.

Is not the trajectory of the alphabet through its
brokenness? The letters learned then broken,
cruelly, into ever changing groups, not friending
one another, but ever changing? Seeing each other
now & then again in certain sentence structures?

Indian art is kinetic.

Our Hope is still in horses, in their movement.
In the migration through the human condition.
Its diversities & relationships
gathering strength, courage, dignity.

With art saying Now Hear This.

We get down to our bones in art.
We find they're the bones of others.
In this there's communication between the
ethnic groups.

& in this there's also the separation.
Why did I wake one morning with the thought
the bridge I'm trying to write about is
different from the grounds it tries to span?

Is it that maybe cultural bridges don't exist?
Maybe there's a reality in the Tower of Babel
& we are heirs of a divine separation.

But I'm a cultural bridge.
I would negate myself if I believed that.
Yet it seems that art is that discovery.
A discovery I didn't want after all.

October \
From the Back Screen of the Country

I think I'm always trying to break thru the prairie into pockets of the world around me. It's because, even as I write, I still hear my mother's voice, don't leave the yard.

I search for diversity on the flat space of prairie where I feel enclosed. I make rigid blocks of imagery, which I try to transcend. Ordinary life & imagination are the tools.

But what of ordinary experience which is the frame? & where is this place from which I write? Not Midwest nor Southwest. The Great Plains. Possibly the Midlands. What else could it be called? & what am I doing here?

I was born in the middle of America. Some of my ancestors migrated by choice, some came during the forced march of the Cherokees to Indian Territory. Two generations later, my mother left the farm in Kansas, & my father left Arkansas. These two different people met, became my parents, & stuck it out. Later, I married & didn't. What could there be in our lives to provoke words? Especially the words of poetry: bearer of our cultures, mirror, road map, & releaser of emotions?

I raised two children, finished an education, divorced. I am burdened with rent & groceries, all the things my parents were burdened with. I groan as they groaned. But I will survive. It's the swale that runs through the land: depressions from wagon wheels moving west on the dining floor of the prairie. There's a memory of the trail & its hardships. Not a place for comfort, my mother said of the farm, long after the dust of those trails settled. My father never spoke of his upbringing, except to say that no one gave him anything, & it's true. Except maybe the Lord who blessed his path, & he never knew it.

This is a harsh land. Raw. A place everyone overlooks. Who'd want to come here? Isolated. Empty. 110° in the summer. Blizzardous out on the plains in winter. Narrow. Fundamental. Lonely as poetry itself.

In the early mornings, I sit on the back steps of my beige bungalow. I can tell by the chipped paint, the house used to be seagreen. Somewhere in memory, almost two thousand miles from either coast, boats float over the water like quilting needles on the farm.

It's much like the house where I grew up, which my parents owned. I rent. A backward step, a not-doing-as-well. A letting myself over the sea wall.

I hear rain on the leaves of the large old trees in the neighborhood, not yet soaked thru. I think of writing from the prairie as being in a colander. As I am aligned with the holes, I see the different views thru miniscule openings. Never the whole scene.

The death of both parents, the refining aspects of daily life. The empty bookcases in the house where I grew up. Impressions of experience. The feeling that far away something is happening. The hurt of lives that fall apart, love that doesn't hold. The voice of the Great Spirit. The fretwork of the mind on the rural concept of stay by the wagon & plow your own field. The ordinary life I write about from the harshness, the fullness of this land.

October 10

69   Wlekli ciężkie ksiażki
     Stoł z nich stawiąc i kładli chleb.
     They have dragged out
     Heavy books and made a table of them
     And begun to cut their bread.

     Czeslaw Milosz, 'A Book in the Ruins'
     (*Separate Notebooks*)

     Glerzy spoots of Kansas Sity
     all see weedsy in a week
     we durve,
     return,
     nert weren't ter' go.
     Bud doo.
     We deed the lund
     t'unkel
     a knuckle for the wurst.
     Wurdge doo.
     Berp. Turp tee 2ed.

Nostrum

70   I think now because it is hard to talk \ taking one word as though a cornfield of form & sound \ its substance of combed furrows farther than anyone can see \ how years ago when everyone was in their rooms for the afternoon \ he took a walk \ instead of loving me \ & knowing later he'd drink himself to oblivion or worse \ & the next day after keeping him quiet when he'd wake with a thunderstorm \ coaxing him \ praying gently to the god who made us \ I sat alone claiming breath after his harping in the night \ a harrow from grandpa's farm \ I want now to go back to myself \ say there will be words for the stalk & husk & ears \ the whole cornfield \ the sound of Yoder's Feed Store \ North Fourth \ & all the glories of the universe.

October 12

71   I think I need to say this is a dream, I'm walking at the edge
     of the highway. I need to say what it's like walking here. I
     have time. My cat's at my side holding the covers down.
     Daylight is a memory of a yellowed page that came loose
     from a book, & I'm saying this is what it's like to write. I've
     got part of the story. The rest travels inside, stopping once
     in a while at the depot of these dreams.

October 15

72   Thege's the way of homal for thurs ancests. Hed run thru
Arkansas 4 thur Cibil war. Thurn goed to thezz hills, ribes
in the slumps, thur green riber. Was ter see thurd shed we
courage to go thru. Carried thezd emnies of sulf, anger,
dread, & sense of loss. Spurzing them as they did us. The
invented letter like a squerd.

October 19

73 Writing is the blank look I leave on my face when I go far
away. Though I drive the geese with my stick, I am sweep-
ing the angels together. The bad ones, you see, who need to
be switched, brought to the front again, not disappearing
into the back of the head, but out here, out here, where I
need them so bad.

Enucleation

I like to read the dictionary now & then, not straight thru like a novel, but opening the book to a certain page to look at words as though they were vegetables in a market. The latest word I took is 'enucleate.' 1. To make clear & 2. to heal, as in the removal of a tumor.

So I want to make some 'enucleations,' some points of clarity on the subject of poetry.

1. The origin of a poem should be something like the origin of the universe. After the bang of inspiration, there should be an imbalance of matter & antimatter. After they destroy one another in the initial struggle of getting the poem on the page, there should be some matter left over. That debris, when cooled & solidified, is the 'poem.'

2. Often the ideas I write about come from what is happening in my life. For instance, reading a news article on how scientists are still pondering the origin of life.

3. Poetry should be nuciferous. One of the 'nut-bearing' trees in the garden. It should open knowledge & understanding. It should be getting us all into trouble, then be the healing balm.

4. All good lines are epicyclic like transmission gears. They should be on their own, while hinging on the larger process of the poem. The dictionary definition of epicycle,

'a circle in which a planet moves & which has a center that is itself carried around at the same time on the circumference of a larger circle.' In other words, the line of a poem has its own orbit, yet moves within the purpose of the larger orbit of the poem.

5. Poetry uses the hub of a torque converter for a jello mold. It should always do the unexpected. At times it should attempt the outrageous.

6. Writing lays out the planetary on a table like fish bones. A planetary is a train of gearwheels in a transmission, which I didn't know until I took my car to a garage to see what was wrong with it. Well, they laid out the parts of my transmission on the table & then called me in as next-of-kin. When I saw all those parts, & how worn they had become in the 164,000 miles my car has traveled, I thought how the parts of the poem fuse & work together.

7. The final point of clarity being the strangeness of the poet to the very world the poet heals & clarifies &, yes, even creates.

Furniture

Separate pieces for a single room
      or, What New Horizons Lie

I like to surprise words.
Ask them to do what they're not supposed to.
Just yes I guess embarrass them.

Put them where they don't belong.

Margin writing. I remember it as a child. Writing
in the margins of a book. Just as the Irish poet
visiting said that monks used to write in the
margins of the manuscripts they copied. The
first Gaelic poetry was the notation of a bird
singing as if the scratch-marks of his little feet
walked on the corner of the parchment.
Not the new manuscript no but the one the monk
copied from while he looked out across the heat of
the field and heard the root of thunder. The crop
of air bundled at the window. He'd write the
outpourings of himself right next to the awful
outpourings of God.

Is braithre muid go leir.

Is brothers that all we are.

And when the Irish poet reads Gaelic
you think you hear the word fuckles
and maybe later lawning.

And you remember how you sit sometimes on your porch
and watch your cat smell the brown blossoms
left by other animals in the yard.

And it makes you think how once close to the end of
your marriage when anything was tried how he put his
head to your crotch like the squirrel at the window
eating the crust of bread you offered that winter
trying to break the territory
the closed meaning between two people

Don't try no to figure out
but take the trip get in the vehicle already moving
where language sounds like a marble-game of ghosts

Even the angels a chance to speak
their airy language
maybe lisping or rubbing their tongues irritatingly
over their lips
leaving spittle where words hang out

The animal heaven beginning also
it's them talking to us sometimes
when I hear my cat with her face next to mine
wake me in the morning
her whiskers on my nose
her authority deciding when we should rise
as angels wiping our wings over the bed
chair
table
the other four-leggeds
in the room

I think any moment she will speak hoksila ki
sukawakan a opta but that is my Indian grandmother
or the Irish poet I've mixed i dtitim throm threan
na fearthainne in falling strong heavy of the rains
I tell him how the word-order-different how it
haunts those loose marbles rattling like pencils
on the page phehi huska ki kuwa she finishes her
Indian chant the boy the horse on his shot hair long
the chase
chanted until the braves could ride outnumbered
into battle

And how the language speaks now
namow
a sweater pulled off backwards
something like whamo

It's not easy to speak as women
going not our language the is
and hasn't for a long maybe never
we say to children wordless places

We remember how once we wore a crown of candles
in old Christmas churches
the light of the world on our heads
yet all that going was only wax-droppings in our
hair
blessed be name of us all
while Adam named the animals
what did she do just sit and listen did she not have
words of her own names of the beings other than she
did she just say words that fit another

and say hoksila to the roped-off clouds
Adam ground-given toil
she birth-given child
the whole neighborhood still full of them.

I hear women in their country they inhabit
the circle of their voices like rolls of barbed-wire
on western fence-posts
their words an untilled field
a frontier voice
a west pole

the bopening ellargements
the crying of them from their spilled milk
disrupting the holy ground
tearing up the hedges the fielded rows
this is something you won't want to hear
another apple for you Adam

Is braithre muid go leir
We are all brothers
Not quite

Well but to see a landscape the way a painter does
take notes about the landscape which you will paint
the blue sky a butter-knife
icing the Christmas cookies for the 2:30 party

A grade-school green as winter grass in Oklahoma
A red lawn yes I want it red
A bright blue royal sky as the paint when we made
handprints

O not a room but hopened air
as though it closed and did.
Moving in now the new furniture of words.

80 My pencil says American. The American pencil opens
to all wide windows two doors at least. A higher
ceiling. In my composition the American pencil is a
buffalo. The large leaded eye from old photographs.
Silent as wind in the grass. Silent as my pencil
crossing paper. Well the buffalo of course the act
of writing as annihilation the noisy leak of others
wobbly-as-a-first-bicycle-ride.

Whatdo you think what know your mind
the air-filled empty corners
the first warm breeze after a Minnesota winter
the bird-songue from your beak.

I asked the Irish poet what he thought of Americans
he says the largeness of the country of course
the not knowing of how to be other than first
he says the fear of decision
the not realizing their effect in the world
and the yes concern for right

Is braithre muid go leir.

The process of synthesis is what writing is
the job last learned

and I thought if all the glasses I ever drank from
were lined up

what sink would hold the goblets the peanut-butters
the jellyjars with grinning faces of Howdy Doody
in the base

81   And I think It should be the return of missing
connectives
the out-of-order animal-words ghost-words
angel-words
indivisible and
indecipherable as pastel chalk-marks of children
on the walk

the margins moved to the middle of a clean bright
page.

29th Street, Indianapolis, &
Far Out across the Indiana Fields

82 You'd be surprised if it was not your birthday & someone
came with a gift: a house in which you used to live, the fir
tree grown tall, up over the roof.

Or possibly, the house shriveled under the tree, warping
the step, pulling the door open a little.

Inside, a rug with vermiculated pattern is a contour map of
anger & the rising area of blame.

Or is it a more recent house in which you tried to live with
your husband & children? But the same humps emerged,
pushing the inheritance of rupture into them which they
will carry to their children.

Years later they say they dreamed it was not you waiting at
the door but a monster.

Perhaps it's also grief under the small wavy circles in the
rug, not a smooth rug like in other houses with rows of
zinnias & tidy yards.

You are a steep hill plowed sideways against erosion, hori-
zontal as party streamers on a windy day when it is not
your birthday & you receive a gift, bulging & unasked for.

November 24 \
The Chrome of Passing Fenders

I walked along the river one night & saw lights from the other bank swirling in the current. Van Gogh's Starry Night, or Cypresses & Starry Night, as I have also seen it, came to mind— Stars bursting like poppies! Air currents visible as water currents. A river transplanted to the sky. His vision eased boundaries into one another. The river no longer stayed river, but could be sky. It was a matter of perspective.

The contemporary poem does much the same with a possibly similar motive. Poetry examines an emotional truth. It's an experience filtered through the personality of the poet. We look to poetry for visions, not scientific truths. The poet's job is to combine new elements. Explore their melting, seeping into one another. The metaphor is the building block of the poem. It & sound. Narrative doesn't always do it anymore.

Poetry saves what is human in this world going gaudy & insane. In exploring small truths, something larger might turn up, adding dimension, insight, vision, recognition to our lives. We just might be more complete, more aware after a poem.

Poetry is a way of being. It breaks out of the ordinary because the poet has broken out. That is the motive of perspective. Not the static, but the mobility of life is the reason for transference. A passionate vision no boundary can hold. A breaking thru to the real.

20th century poetry is a piñata. Images break from the earth when the poet strikes it. Emblazing the imagination. Seeds for fertilization so that I can say, this is what I have come to see & believe about this place—this river & sky converging—this past & future, this nothing & everything. See— This is the life I live!

The cemetery on the distant hill looks like small, petrified trees caught with frost.

The cottonwoods of a child's white fingers as we travel north to Kansas City for Thanksgiving with my brother and 2 aunts and an uncle.

Herds of hayrolls in fields, grazing as they are grazed.

Headlights yellow in the fog ahead. Skies roofed with winter. Old cornfields.

Frost on bent stalks of milo, fragmented as the family.

Now the sky is on the earth. A universe of stars sparking in fields. Constellations of them moving along orbits of highway & turnpikes, crossing the country, twirling up country roads.

The 20th century poem is a work of cloisonné, as Van Gogh's work often was, encased in its own boundary of meaning & opulence.

The poet writes as he is written by circumstance & environment.

Across the veined sky.

Our jittery words shuffle to one another.

86   After the divorce, I had new territory, much like the Oklahoma land run when a piece of land was claimed & had to
be settled. I had spent years hiding behind my husband, the
children & housework. Now the land & sky were open.
That's what's frightening about the prairie at first \ its
barrenness & lack of shelter. I had always written, but
now my sense of place was defined by whatever mattered.
I picked up my Indian heritage & began a journey toward ani-yun-wiyu, or, translated from the Cherokee, 'real
people.'

I read journals \ magazines. Poetry \ some fiction. I saw that
feelings could be expressed in writing. Feelings of be-
wilderment & fear. Especially anger. It was a trend in
women's writing \ the pulley I needed out of the separation
& isolation I felt without the surroundings of family. I saw
women come to grips with themselves. The vulnerability,
the struggle, the agonizing choices. I had to find a home-
stead within myself, or invent one. I dug a potato cellar.

Family had covered the fissures in my life. Now I had
fragments \ shards \ whatever the territory offered. My
poems & writing were the land I cultivated. I moved toward 'being' in poetry. A struggle for survival. My purpose
was to find the truth of what I was \ my voice. What I had to
offer. I could not have done it without the other voices \ the
sun & rain & soil for myself as a person. The pleasure of
being a woman.

I found that I weathered the prairie storms & the limitations that come with the territory. I found acceptance of myself \ the strength to travel prairie roads & talk about poetry in towns where farmers in the cafés stare. I relived the struggle to claim the land \ establish a sod house \ plow the fields \ milk the cow. The rest will come. All this is an internal land, of course. I started late with only a map given to me by other women who said the territory was there. It was a fertile landscape just inside the head. I had only to load the wagon, hitch the horses. A journey which my mother never made before she folded up her camp.

I learned to trust images. I could even experiment with words. Put muffler, glass packs on the wagon. Mud flaps if I wanted. I have what men have had \ liberty to be myself. Maybe women had it too & I just never knew. Wrong \ wright \ whatever. Now I could throw out the ice cubes \ find my severed limbs \ sew them on instead of giving heart & arms & lungs away. I have use for them on the edge of the frontier \ saw-edge after saw-edge.

The glory of the plain self in search of words to say, 'the self' \ the delight of it. The birth \ the shedding of invisibility. The pursuit of she-pleasure. SHEDONISM.

The themes \ form \ experimental forms. Words as house & shed & outbuildings on the land. The urgency. The cessation of pounding myself \ hanging my separate parts to dry on low branches & rocks. It's women who influenced my work. Their courage \ their trend toward revelation. I am on the journey to the ani-yun-wiyu.

Astoria Boulevard

88   The cab passes a Christmas tree lot in Queens. A man
arranges fir trees and wreaths, his hands the size of postal
cards in fir boughs. A glimpse of him caressing trees, and
those asleep on park benches along Astoria Boulevard, is
all there is time for. The scrawl of graffiti decorates subway
tracks on the way to La Guardia. Strings of lights and
ornaments brought from attics are stiff as the cold that
hovers near barrel-fires. The tree-seller warms his hands,
picks a tree for the Astoria Baptist Church in the Christ-
child season when hope rises like planes over the neighborhood and sends smothered messages to those asleep, small
as hands.

Claiming Breath

89 How do you begin writing poetry? I would say after all these years I'm not sure. First of all, you read. You have to be aware of what's being written. Poetry is a conversation. Often while I'm reading, I start a poem. An image will set off another image, or I think of something I want to say.

It also helps to know the tradition of poetry, though often there's something about it that gets in the way. You strain for a rhyme without thought for the fire, the energy of the poem, the originality of voice. Yet I've heard others say that structure forces them to work in ways they would have missed on their own.

Begin by getting words down. What have you got to say? Even if you want to remain obscure there has to be coherence on some level. I remember hearing Gerald Stern say, if you get your words in order on the first row, you make room for a craziness later on, deeper in the poem, in a more important place.

Work with what you've experienced. I think sometimes, who cares about my ordinary life? But often, that's exactly what matters.

What idea, impression, image, do you want to convey? Why should I listen to you? Again, 1) read, 2) write what you have to say, & 3) read it to someone. Listen to their reaction, their criticism, & write again. So much of writing is rewriting.

Contemporary poetry says what you have to say in whatever way you want to say. Make sure you have a style, a voice, a certain way of expressing yourself. Where's your uniqueness, your individuality? You have a thumbprint different from other thumbprints. You have a way of seeing & a way of expressing what you see that is also different. Develop that difference. Take chances with unusual words & combinations. Writing is a long process. Reveal what it's like to be you.

Do you have something bothering you? Get into it. That will save the trouble of writing boring poems.

Remember imagery, the mental pictures your writing makes, usually thru metaphor & simile. Make sure they haven't been said before. They have to be new. Tell me something in a way I haven't heard it before. Let an image connect with a thought, sometimes a memory. Get rid of weak verbs. Watch tenses, make them consistent. Use DETAIL! A cotton dress printed with crocuses is usually better than 'a dress.' Look for the right word. The inevitable one. Ask what your poem means. What conclusion is drawn from it? Even if not a logical thought, but an impression. Good poems are sometimes simple, on at least one level.

What is life like for you? That's what you should begin writing about.

Remember also the richness of language. Make sure there's a lot in your writing. Read your words to yourself. Listen to them on a tape recorder.

The form a poem takes on the page is also integral. Experiment with line breaks, stanzas, the square or prose poem, the words wiggling over the page.

91 Then workshop a poem. Critiques are usually common sense. Does the poem work? Do you like it? Does it begin at the first stanza or do you really get into the poem several lines later? Do all the parts form a whole? What central thought holds the poem together? What emotion or impression is shared? What stays in your mind after you've heard it? Is it in the form it should be in? Is the poem clear? Have you said the same thing too many times? Is the reader rewarded for reading it?

Be interested in a lot of things. Be an interesting person, live a responsible life. Start keeping notes.

I think it's also important to know why you write. When I go into a bookstore & see shelves full of books, I think why do I do this? Hasn't it been done better than I can do it? That's when I have to be able to look in myself & decide, I have something to say too— These other books can move over & make room for mine.

Invention

92 I came to the end of human experience. Married, divorced, children raised, parents buried. What would I do now? Discover another letter of the alphabet? One that comes between *m* & *n*?

A thought flies into my head. What if discovery is beyond me? Maybe the new letter has to be invented. Something that looks like **ɱ** ?

Yes, 27 is a better number than 26. The letters of the alphabet would not have equilibrium.

And weren't they too close anyway—*m* & *n*? The new letter changes combinations, the way a turn of an old kaleidoscope shifts patterns. I work with its capital. Its cursive.

I spend ages again learning, discovering, inventing, making mistakes & carrying on despite obstacles. My new letter changes the sound of other letters, confounding the English language more than it already is. The foreigner goes bananas.

I love the words I write with the new letter. They become my children. Eager for my attention, they wait in rows on the page. Now I am worth listening to, like Aunt Yulda who used to read to me. There was no boredom when we were together. There was a fusion of purpose & understanding. A struggle for balance. Everything life is about.

A Hogan in Bethlehem

93 & so it was in a country across the water, she gave birth to a
son & wrapped him in a buffalo robe. The raccoon & elk &
deer gathered in the hogan-manger. & there were shepherds, or animal-watchers, in the field, & lo, an angel, a
spirit-being with wings, a bird-person, appeared the way a
coyote or tumbleweed crosses the headlights on a reservation road at night. & the high-beam of Wakan Tanka, the
Great Spirit, shined as if all the campfires of the stars
burned at once. & the animal-watchers, the shepherds,
were afraid. But the angel said, fear not, for the news is
good. Unto all people this night is born a Chief who is
Wovoka, Christ our Lord. & suddenly there were other angels & hosts of spirit-beings in war-paint & feathers shouting their war-cries & praising Wakan Tanka, the Great
Spirit, who had sent a Chief to walk among us. Though
still a baby he would be the light for our darkness. He
would be the sustenance for our lives. & the angels & war-
beings chanted glory in heaven & on earth, a peace-pipe.
Then all the spirit-beings flew back to heaven, & the elk &
deer & caribou returned to the woods, & the Wovoka baby
slept in the manger. Meanwhile, 3 scouts, 3 Medicine Men,
made their vision-quest under one star still burning like a
yard-light on the prairie. As if the Great Spirit didn't want
to leave the baby, or in case the baby wanted to migrate
back from earth. So the Medicine Men hurried with their
bundle-gifts to find a hogan in Bethlehem. They hurried to
find the Wovoka-child wrapped like a holy ear of corn.

A Confession or
Apology for Christian Faith

How could I believe this stuff? A white child in a manger.
How often have I heard the Indian way vs. the Christian?
Yet the old ways are lost to me. So many of them I've heard
are similar to Christianity anyway. Stories of animals talking about the cruelty of man. The bird because he is im-
paled on a stick over a fire until his feet & feathers are
burned off. The deer because he is dragged thru the woods
by his antler & not thanked for his life. Something had to
be done. In some myths, disease was our punishment, but
there wasn't really an answer, a propitiation.

There is also a Coyote story of Coyote himself confessing
his sins before he died one of his many deaths. After which
he only comes back to trick again. But there is this vague
notion that something is wrong & what can be done to
right that wrong? Possibly the Great Spirit is 'the other' &
we are trying to connect with him. Maybe because we
chose our own way instead of his. & God is somehow up
there with the stars, & we are here. How can the gap be
closed? By our own works? Isn't it part of many ceremonies
to suffer & be worthy? Isn't there a general feeling of alien-
ation?

It's possible the various drawings on teepees & teepee lin-
ings, & the intricate body markings & hair ornaments &
costume beading could be called an attempt at salvation. A
reminder to both the Great Spirit & the Indian of the
Indian's worth. It seems to me anyway that a sense of
worth needed to be recorded. A stave against darkness.

The sun dance could also be something of a salvation attempt. The brave is attached to a pole by means of skewers
hooked thru the pectoral muscles. He pulls back on the
skewers until they rip loose from his muscles, & he is free
from the post. But the dance doesn't have the finality of the
cross. It is repeated when the brave needs to prove his
worth or make some intercession for the tribe.

Then there's the tradition, when some loved one died, of
making 2 cuts in your arm & thrusting a twig in the loop of
flesh so blood would flow. Doesn't this custom seem to
hint at redemption also? A sign of mourning which Christianity finished with its emphasis on the bloodshed of
Christ.

There are other stories of similarities between Biblical &
Native events that made it easier for me to believe. I think
in Pretty Shield's tales there's a story of an old warrior
woman who rode into battle with a root-digger, shouting
that the enemy was on the run. I think of Samson fighting
with the jawbone of an ass & the Israelites circling the wall
of Jericho, shouting for it to fall. It's a matter of faith in
both traditions. The power of our words.

Christ's wilderness experience could be called a vision
quest. & aren't there similarities in the Native American
naming ceremony & in Biblical accounts, from Adam
naming the animals to the Annunciation? Stories of the
flood & dispersement of the people afterwards are held in
common too.

Did you know that Christ also has a secret name? 'And his
eyes were like a flame of fire, & on his head were many

crowns; & he had a name written, that no man knew, but he himself'—Revelation 19:12. '& he was clothed with a vesture dipped in blood; & his name is called The Word of God. & the armies that were in heaven followed him upon white horses, clothed in fine buckskin (linen), white & clean. & out of his mouth goeth a sharp spear (sword) that with it he should smite the nations, & he shall rule them with a rod of iron; & he treadeth the winepress of the fierceness & wrath of Almighty God. & he hath on his ghost shirt (vesture) & his thigh a name written, Chief of Chiefs & Lord of Lords.'—Revelation 19:13–16.

Christ wears body paint? He goes for tattoos? When I read of the writing on his thigh, I see war-paint.

Maybe even the peace pipe could be a type of Christ. Maybe it's similar to the burnt offering in the Tabernacle in the Old Testament. & with the belief that the smoke of the peace pipe is the breath of the Great Spirit, comes the thought that Christ is present in the elements of communion.

And how about the belief in supernatural beings & ghosts? It's in the form of the Holy Ghost that God's Spirit is manifest after the cross. In the Native American tradition, the supernatural is more linked to nature, the feather carried in the medicine bundle, for instance, or the vision of whatever animal loaned its power.

Then there's also the idea of tolerance & acceptance in the Indian as well as the Christ-mind. & we have need for acceptance of others. Did not the coming of the white man force diversity on the Indian? Isn't that the struggle those-who-came have inherited? I think I've heard that by the year 2020 the minorities of this country will be in the majority.

97   & why not Christian faith? The white man brought the gun & horse, two beloved possessions. Why not also a spirit message, a finish to the animals talking of the problem of wrong? Even though it seems the white man no longer believes his own creed. Faith in Christ to make me whole & forgiven. It's the way I feel sometimes. The incarnation of the Spirit in the flesh. Wakan Tanka as one of us so we can become one of him by faith in the Christ born in a hogan in Bethlehem.

Christ as the great Chief. 'He that is greatest among you shall be your servant.'—Matthew 23:11. Isn't the Chief of the tribe the one who must give the most away? Even his life. Could the cross be called the ultimate give-away?

I need to say here the hardest thing to say. I think the sacred hoop of the Indian nation was broken because it wasn't the sacred hoop of God. It wasn't complete. It left too much to pride & self works.

'There is a way which seemeth right to man but the end thereof are the ways of death.'—Proverbs 14:12.

The fulfillment of God's way & not ours. & the incompleteness of the sacred hoop before God was made evident. & it was broken by the white man with his terrible ways. His repeating rifles & broken treaties & all the treachery that is in the human heart.

Yet in that imperfect vehicle came news of the light. That is a hard lesson. Maybe it's easier if the Indian traditions are seen as a type of the Old Testament. & Christianity is a fulfillment of the old ways. But who can be fulfilled without the star quilts on the church walls, the burning of cedar at the altar, & the drum hymns?

So be quiet now. Let the Wovoka baby sleep. Let him grow in our hearts & do what he must. I need him anyway in the long struggle toward the light.

Dance Lessons with the Spirit World

99   I just found out where the woman was when Adam named the animals. She wasn't yet. It was afterwards she came from his rib. He even named her woman because she came from-him or afterhim or underhim. How can I believe this stuff?

I'll take the back seat anyway & drive. Who cares? What else am I here for? I just interrupted my writing to go to the store for birdseed on this cold day. I have a feeder in the back yard & when it's empty & the ground is snowy, the birds sit in it & look at my window.

I think awareness of nature & the unseen world is inherent in the Native American.

It's not always a positive world. There's the coyote trick-ster tradition in which you end up with nothing. In fact, you are nothing. So is existence & the Great Spirit himself. That's the ultimate trick. No matter what you do, & how often you do it, there's really nothing to do.

I hear echoes of it in literary theory. The word cannot mean the object. Signifier & Signified are in 2 different worlds. The woman is also other, or that which is not-quite-man. An afterman.

No wonder the birds have their seed to eat.

Life is a dance of illusion & there is no reality. The word does nothing but manifest our nothingness. In fact, speech itself is a separator.

& in the end, you bring your harvest, the work of your hands, & it is rejected. All your works are nothing.

But there is a brother. Another side. The spoken word empowered to codify our existence. In fact, it even speaks existence. Did not God speak the world into being in the book of Genesis? We speak our lives into being by the shape & intent of our words.

It was the other brother who brought a lamb to the Lord. A blood sacrifice. & his offering was accepted. But he got killed. Just like the man in the other Testament.

Anyway.
Is there a reality beyond what we see?
Is dying some sort of unfolding in another way?
Is coyote out-coyotied after all?
Do we have meaning or are we recipients of a trick?
& even with meaning, do we end up anywhere?

How long have we been asking these questions?

I think you can say Native American spirituality is a necessity because we lost nearly everything that defined our culture. The hunt. Migration. Buffalo. Story. Life as it was.

Thus belief is important.
Faith often means survival.
Belief in circumstances which are not yet present.
It helps us over loss.

At one time I believed because I had to. My life & those of my children depended upon a positive attitude. We would survive. We spoke the words of survival & those words made our world come into being. The Great Spirit was the insurer of it. We spoke words that echoed his words & together they made some sort of implosion, some sort of phenomenology.

The way was made & we walked it.
It was there as long as we said it was
& put our feet on it.
A kaleidoscopic piece of dry ground in the midst
of chaos.

Maybe it's not there for someone else.

But now my life is easier.
As I sit watching
the birds.
The candles on the tin Christmas tree burning.
My daughter in law school,
my son a Marine Lieutenant in the Persian Gulf.

I can look at the word as coyote & say the word
as coyote doesn't exist.

Possibly.

Didn't we survive?
To face further death anyway.

What I say gives meaning to what I say it to.

It's the written word also I will add. It's my mother's hand-
writing that is most real now that she's dead. In 2 of her

pitchers I inherited, she has written who gave them to her
& in what year. I feel her there in the act of her writing.

I think in blessing words we entertain angels
unaware. I think that means angels unaware
they're angels.

Who but words can put us in our place?
The Great Spearers.
Broken from the Great Spearer himself.

So our words don't equal their object.
So we don't equal God.
There are spiritual implications of
deconstructionism.
Beginning with the loss, & recognition of that
inherent failure, that fallen-shortness,
that tail of beginning defined by what we are not.

Our life is a migration of tribal separations-from, until we
face the Great Nothingness, the Great Coyote & say to
him who we think we are.

The Nail-down of Oral Tradition

Oral tradition carries the fire, the spirit of the people. It's an invisible library. A personal and tribal identity. Without the definition of inner life that oral tradition gives, our people are open to a sense of purposelessness.

We don't stand up well against the Vacuum.

We need to know our culture. Otherwise we don't know who we are, where we came from. We need that 'sense of being' that oral tradition carries. If we do not have a sense of belonging to 'tribe' and at the same time a sense of being an individual within that group, we miss what it is 'to-be.'

For centuries our stories were passed in oral tradition. The voice is more important than the written word. The Great Spirit created man because He wanted communication. The animals were not capable of providing it, neither the elements. He wanted us with our free wills and our voices praising His creation, thanking Him for life. He wanted us to tell stories about our place in the world, stories that carried fundamental truths of how to live and the consequences of wrong deeds. He wanted us to speak of hope sustained even through death into the afterlife.

With written language came the task of learning how to hammer the voice onto the page with these little nails called 'alphabet.' For many Native Americans it's only been a matter now of two generations.

For some reason I'm stuck on the point of clarity when I think of Native American writing. Maybe I'm speaking more to myself than others. I know that poetry should have mystery. It should resist the intelligence, as I have heard somewhere. But maybe that 'resistance' should be on another level. Not at the core of meaning, but in the interaction of parts on their inroads to our sensibilities. Sometimes I want to know what's happening in a poem. Especially since I think one of the jobs of the Native American writer is the preservation of myths that are being forgotten.

Maybe the answer is that the reader cannot ask for the preservation of all myths in words. Maybe they are something to be guarded within the tribe. But the myths still might be safer stored in the written word, even the English written word. The Spirit world protects itself. 'Those-who-do-not-see' or 'those-who-are-not-supposed-to-see' could read without understanding.

But there's still the possibility that besides preservation and restoration and communication (as if that wasn't enough), the Native American poet's job also is to provide new myths by which we survive this world. The poet should experience the white world and bring forth what he is in it. He should be a visionary giving strength to the people. He should record how life is possible in this alien

world. Where are the map makers along with the protes-
tors? Surely we can survive this wilderness too. A record-
ing of the myths that are dying in practically every culture
seems a right step. And since there is such a vast difference
between the tribes, I want clarity.

Our world is both a part-anthropomorphic, part–deus ex
machina world with the different parts bleeding into one
another. It's part magic, part horror. A quasi-solid, floating,
changing and uncohesive world. No wonder it is so difficult to see clearly.

Not only is it difficult to deal and connect with this new
world, often we don't connect with our old one either. So
much of it is gone and what's left is often frightening.

Once when my brother and I were alone for an evening, we
heard a chair move upstairs. We looked at one another,
then went on with our game. I often have the feeling I share
my space with the spirits.

Maybe I should take for granted that things move around,
nothing holds to its boundaries, and things come out dif-
ferently with each telling, when I ask for clarity.

I could say the Indian is the voice of the Spirit in this world.
Except I walked to the post office too many times in down-
town Tulsa and passed the drunks sitting on the street in
front of the library, or standing in the middle of the side-
walk arguing over which bus to get on.

Some of the Indian voices are destructive and fearful.
Maybe instead of the voice of the Great Spirit alone, the

Indian is the voice of the spirit world and all its forces, good and evil. We know some angels fell out of heaven (or were thrown out, as the story goes). The Indian seems to stand in this doorway to the other realm.

It's a place I've always been aware of. Many times when I've called out to the Great Spirit I've been spared. When my marriage was difficult and finally ended, when I sent my children out on their own, when I face loneliness and depression and concern for my old age. How will I have money? How could I live so long without accumulating anything other than some pieces of furniture and a few books? Yet the assurance of the Great Spirit is always there. Somehow we survive.

PART THREE: GETTING TO WHAT I
WANT TO TALK ABOUT (SATURDAY NIGHT RADIO)

What is it to be Indian, or part Indian, removed by generations & space from that heritage? The language dead. The culture severed. It should have little effect. But my sense of place in the Midwest is defined by that land that was—the vast prairies & our migration over them. It is also defined by a sense of language which is lost.

Sometimes there's an old voice in my head. Not a voice that enters the ear, except when he chants. But even then it's my voice that his rides upon. No, his voice is one I feel in Spirit. Have not radio waves carried into space & returned to earth years later? How much more a human Spirit? Especially one who dies from grief. Not a ghost, no, but a living voice that says his people are sick and without food. The snow is deep & cold hangs on. Maybe the Great Spirit sees them. Maybe when the moon dies, He will take them to the Hunting Grounds from the long trail they march.

I tell the old Grandfather it is over. Why is he grieving? Did not some of us survive the trail to the new territory? Did not the Cherokee translate hymns & the Bible with Sequoya's syllabary? Are not our stories & legends & myths replaced by faith in the living God of this nation?

I follow him into his grief. It's a large brown box I enter—as if an old radio—the kind that once stood in the corner of the living room like a buffalo. I hear the wireless transmissions of electric impulses converted into sound. Is it not Christ we see with our faith? Is it not Him who walks over the moving sludge of the world? Sometimes the arms reaching up to Him are snakes. But He speaks peace to them. Quaddo. Words are the body. The Spirit made visible. Not just a code. Oh, no. The word is not a mirror of the object, is not the object, but a making of the object into the shape of the tribe— Maybe even the Spirit Himself. That's what speaks & carries into the captivity of knowledge.

When we talk we jump-start the electromagnetic field of language. Moving waves of speech. How else do we keep ourselves from extinction? How else do we make room for ourselves as we're crowded out? Nothing left as we knew it after the transmutation of our world.

But I am without his words when I talk. You know the language of my ancestors didn't survive. A radio full of static. Once we had the reception of signals. I still hang on to what floats over the land like a stray herd—the sound waves of the ancestors that sewed the tribe together—but there was raveling of that gravity—a scissoring out of language like a gutted carp, the fish eggs of vapor drops from the journey. It's like being a space man floating in air— Suddenly the hose is severed— You whizz backward through space. That's what it's like to have no language. You are without the means to convey what you think.

Often I have the feeling my speech moves along one trail, while my thoughts follow another.

I remember listening to Saturday-night radio when I was a girl, my face pushed to the speakers. Inside I could see the faint lights of the tubes like red campfires of a migrating tribe. They are still locked in that darkness & part of me is in there with them. I am always aware of the Indian tribes that crossed our land—following herds or migrating to summer camp.

When I was growing up my father worked for the stockyards in Kansas City. Later he was transferred to other cities in the Midwest. He left his heritage to follow this world & I remember the vacuum it made in him. Our heritage doesn't die— It leaves an open gash in need of stitches. Riding in the back seat of our '49 Ford, I watched his black hair—his hands on the wheel. I remember feeling the universe there with us—& at the same time, I remember the hole in our heads where our heritage had once been. The large white moon shined over us like an eye in the afternoon sky & we were left with pieces of stars we couldn't yet see.

If you don't have words, you don't have your world. How do you shoot an antelope or jack rabbit without the hunting-sign of the language that captures the animal & says, animal you are mine? How do you tie together your truth & the experience which goes against it? How do you make tolerable a world which is not?

Once when the back of the radio was open for repair, I lost that sense of an Indian camp. Then I saw the tubes as they were—a city of the plains as it would look to the ancestors if they could have seen the lighted buildings, the surreal grain silos & storage towers, the domes & terminals that would stand up on the prairie.

But it's Christ, remember Christ we saw under the moaning & wailing—under the agonies we know. I thump the old voice in my head. I say hey, you, old Grandfather—Sing! Sing your song.

What's left otherwise but hollow sounds? We speak our world into being with what we have. We make up the words which hold what happens. We learn to speak our meanings with these new words of English. Maybe the old ones wait for us somewhere. Otherwise we're transmitters in space sending signals no one receives.

Now I tell the old Grandfather I have to hang the washing on the line—I have to live in this world. I use the stars as clothespins— All night my dreams ripple on the line like sheets until I take them in at morning— But the moon—leave it there to shrivel—thinking how it is barren because it is so white.

The Indian tribes are vastly different. My tribe, the Cherokee, was a domestic, woodland tribe. They were corn farmers, mill owners, fur & skin traders in Tennessee, Georgia & the Carolinas, until removal to Indian Territory west of the Mississippi. We had none of the glorious exploits & migrations of the Plains & Southwest Indians. In the Cherokee capital of Tahlequah, Oklahoma, today, you hear concern for economic stability. The work ethic & the Christian faith were the foundations of my upbringing in Kansas City. Back in 1821, when Sequoya invented his syllabary, the first translations into Cherokee were the book of John & a few Christian hymns. The Phoenix, the Cherokee newspaper, is in print today. The new way to write language also recorded the myths & stories of our pre-Christian oral tradition. That tradition in all tribes is vital. What would you be without your books? What would you be if you had no resource or reference material when you went to write your papers? & what if you lost your driver's license, social security number, your address & name? & new ones were issued in a language you couldn't understand? That's what sudden acculturation must be. It didn't go too well.

But when tribes were forbidden to speak their native language, as happened in reservation schools, & this oral tradition was forgotten, the human without his sense of culture, his spirit, emerged. Having one's language stripped is like having one's skin removed. Anything can get in. Alcoholism among all tribes is common. It results from the loss of culture, & personal & tribal identity. A sense of purposelessness follows. All because the oral tradition is severed. Does not the Bible say 'My people are destroyed for the lack of knowledge'? (Hosea 4:6).

Being of 2 cultures (my mother was white), & having those cultures divided within themselves between Christianity & superstition & myth, & Christianity itself divided among interpretations, & myths & superstitions divided among versions, there's much to choose from. Compare creation stories: Once there were animals living on a piece of land until the land grew crowded. One animal was pushed off in search of new land. He dove into a body of water, & brought mud back to the surface. When it dried, the animals inhabited it too. Man came later, crawling out of a log in some tales, of unclear origin in others. The other creation story of course: In the beginning God created heaven & earth & the land was without form & eventually God said, 'Let the dry land appear.'

In the Cherokee tradition, there are also 'little people' tales. Children must watch out & not get pulled into one of their holes. There are 'fables' or 'explanation tales' that enliven one's imagination. (Why all beavers are brown or another instance: The Milky Way is a bag of stolen cornmeal spilled when the robber fled to space.) There are also stories of animal transformations: Grandma was sick in bed. An owl kept hooting in a tree. Papa went out & shot the owl. When he came back, grandma was dead with a bullet hole in her side. That story tells the link between the animal & human worlds. What happens to them, happens to us. Even though I know the point, I still find the possibility of travel into an animal's body disturbing.

112   The Cherokee were settled in Indian Territory (later Oklahoma) by 1840, long before the wars of white soldiers & settlers against the plains Indians, which ended in 1890 with the Ghost Dances at Pine Ridge. The Cherokee never saw a buffalo nor reservations. We had an easier time of it. In Oklahoma there are still pockets where only Cherokee is spoken, & other traditions, such as the Sweat Lodge & the lighting of the Keetowah bonfire, survive. But when I go back and visit an old Cherokee friend near Stilwell, Oklahoma, we talk about scripture. His name is Reverend Ketcher. Now he worries that the young Indians, besides losing their culture, their interest in school, are also losing interest in Christianity. When he was young, everyone hung around the church. Now they don't. What's left? He asks. We need to know who we are, & who we came from. We need our books. We need to be connected to knowledge of some sort or we're like the cave man somewhere in the night without his fire. Again (Proverbs 29:18), 'Where there is no vision the people perish.'

I may make some Native Americans who read this mad. I'm not militant. I'm content to sit in my room & write. I don't want to tear down. Aren't the whites doing that by themselves? They've poisoned the water & land. They're overrunning themselves. Maybe the Ghost Dance will return when we have to ask for an exit, a return to the way things were. Maybe we'll soon long for the Hunting Grounds where we will see the Ancestors & our lives as they should be. I think there's a place we go. I hear it in my bones. For me it's through the Great Chief with the nail holes in his hands. Did not the ancestors see him at Pine Ridge? (I'm also thinking of the peyote visions of Mountain Wolf Woman.) If I got anything from the white man, it's the Christian faith. That's what writing is: we come to grips with the world in our own way. I read many I don't agree with. & they're saying it well. I've received much from this foreign occupation (which will be 500 years in 1992.) Education, plane flight. Anger is included along with dismay that a race capable of moon flight doesn't know how to care for the soil under their feet. Maybe they will learn to Ghost Dance too.

PART FIVE: THE LAST: ORAL TRADITION MADE VISIBLE

The War Chief's children eat stories of their past. \ They swallow fragments of brave deeds, \ buffalo hunts & counting coup. \ The Spirits of their Grandfathers stir. \ A feeling behind a rib \ or under a molar where the root divides. \ The War Chief's children eat stories \ year after year. \ They open their hands in the 5 directions. \ They have a sense of what it is to be. \ The stories fill the whole cavity of the human soul.

PART SIX: NOW THE LAST

When the word disappears the thing disappears.
When our way of talk disappears, we disappear.
Susan Stewart, 'The Last Man'
(*American Poetry Review*, September–October 1988)

Now wait. I read 'The War Chief's Children' and think, where are the 2 things happening at once? Where are the

113

complexities of poetry? The Threading and Unthreading. The sense of discovery, of showing a gentle revelation that's a conduit to fire? Where's the life-stuff of Real Poetry? The use of words for something other than themselves? Where's the pounding sound that drives blood into its little tubes? No flat statements or artifice riding a simple line. Where is the energy of the spirit world? Where's the real stuff of Indian writing that can stand up to words like, 'Each poem, like a saltimbanque—isolated, archaic, and urbane at once—comes forth to present or enact the relation of language to understanding'? (I'm quoting again from Susan Stewart's APR article on John Ashbery.) Could she read 'War Chief's Children' and say 'Swapping purity, disinterestedness for depth, engagement, is precisely the business . . .'? No. Could she say anything at all from that article about any Native American poems?

We have the power. When I was finishing my M.F.A. at the University of Iowa in the fall of 1988, the last semester I drove 300 miles from St. Paul on Mondays for an afternoon workshop. Afterwards I drove the 300 miles back. At times the spirit world was so close I felt I could keep driving. That's the energy, the transcending force available to us. I want it in Native American poetry.

PART SEVEN: RENASCENCE

Mother \ what shall I do with these fins of my feet? They're not suitable. & your daughter's lips bulge gaa gaa \ the large bubbles look quizzically for air. What shall I do? Something wooly sticks to my side. My round eyes see from the sides of my head! They're yellow-ringed \ lovely \ but I'm corralled in these little pools with 2 eyes that used to be ears. There are places inside me full of air. Why am I here? Remember my arms? Now a tight buckskin holds the shaft of my spine \ the thin barbs of lesser bones. I'm all silvery. I jump sometimes from the water to see myself before I splash. But the surface breaks disconnected shapes \ half teepees open to the sky \ little waves moving like a herd. I try & call your name \ I must be careful Mother. A spear cuts the water if I swim near the surface. A hook waits in the dark. Mother \ I'm adjusting. I'm a new wife of God in his hatcheries \ the eggs swell from my body \ the ooze sprays over them. I would not tell you these things but I know you love me. I'm a concubine in a beaded dress. Remember how beautiful \ the circle dance? I'm afraid the old ways didn't last. If I could just get out of the river \ but my polished scales would shrivel in the air \ the yellow rings on my eyes would crinkle. The sky is pulled down to the choppy surface here \ the water feels less frightful in my lungs.

PART EIGHT: AT THE POW WOW GROUNDS

I'm Felina \ little wise chop of the underguard \ dancing in the spirit. \ Hoche. Hoche. \ Feel the smooch of fir boughs. \ The precise bon-bonds, dear Chief. \ Hear their hot specks swill \ the channel of the canoe for kitty brittle. \ I'm the tops, tots. \ No skin off my elbow \ if you want to knock your door closed. \ All I saw is \ these Hymbian totems \ this renascent self. \ I believe I'm here, disappeared and back. \ I want a library in a bundle. \ Fax, man \ this God head up there \ this re-written self \ I've got to see.